Scratching the Surface

by Mark Wheeller

Scratching the Surface

ISBN 978-0-9575659-2-0
First edition published in 2016 by Pping Publishing.
Updated and reprinted in 2016.

A CIP catalogue record for this book is available from The British Library

Printed and Bound by Bookprinting UK
Coltsfoot Drive, Woodston, Peterborough

First Published in Great Britain in 2016
by Pping Publishing
Southampton, Great Britain

Acknowledgements

"Rob" and his family for their words.

The Alderbrook cast for their words and time spent rehearsing and their skills in presenting the play.

Anna Allen for the initial idea, commission and her hugely talented direction of the original production.

Tim Ford (Artistic Director of Lichfield Garrick Theatre) for his ideas and support on the "Inspiration Days"!

Big Lottery Fund (Awards for All, England) for offering the sponsorship to make the play happen.

Solihull Mind & LifeSIGNS

Hazel Howlett - Front cover design

Sonia Oliver Photography – Alderbrook Photos

Clive Hulme – Book Design

Sophie Gorell Barnes,
MBA Literary Agents Limited,
62 Grafton Way,
London W1P 5LD

Tel 020 73872976
Email Sophie@mbalit.com

You may also try wheellerplays@gmail.com
(note the 2 e's and 2 L's) should there be any problems contacting the above.

Foreword by the original director

'Scratching the Surface' has been, for me, one of those rare career and life changing experiences that consumes you, without you realising that life will never quite be the same. The name Mark Wheeller is as common to Drama teachers far and wide, as Mary Berry is to the army of apron clad housewives throughout the land. So when I first sent an email to him back in June 2015 with an idea for a commission, I really didn't expect a reply...but there it was inboxed and waiting by the time I woke up the next day. And that, has been a reflection of my relationship with Mark ever since!

This project has been a very different experience to the usual offering the Alderbrook Drama Department produce in the Spring Term. In June 2015, I applied for a Big Lottery grant to commission Mark to write a verbatim play surrounding the issue of self-harm in young people. The aim of the project was to challenge the stigma attached to self-harm, raise awareness and most importantly open dialogue and highlight local support. Through the dynamic medium of Theatre in Education we wanted to confront the hard-to-reach subject of self-harm head on and to challenge inflexible or ill-informed mindsets. The story of the play at this point was to be based solely on that of 'Rob', an ex-Alderbrook student who had self-harmed during his time with us, his experiences and that of his family during this difficult and life changing period. In late August, we were informed the bid had been successful and, by mid-October, we welcomed Mark to Solihull to interview the family on Day 1 and then lead a workshop session with the would-be ensemble on

Day 2. Day 2 was a revelation for both Mark and I, as the cast spoke of their knowledge and experiences of self-harm amongst their friends. Our eyes and ears were opened, as Mark comments in the play "this experience of talking to you has been remarkable. I had no idea there was this kind of passion behind this topic". We had clearly struck upon an issue which the company themselves had very strong opinions about and Mark decided to cleverly weave this into the structure of the finished play. So, what we end up with essentially is a play within a play.

The ensemble and I continued to meet once a week after this initial workshop day with Mark, even though we had no script to work from! Instead we worked on some of the physical / abstract work you will find embedded in the opening, we looked closely at self-harm research and we studied extracts of work from Mark's previous plays so we could get used to his very specific style of theatre. Our first draft of the script was in late November; a momentous day as we read through those first few pages together and realised we were the caretakers of something very special. It was at this point that I contacted the charities Solihull Mind and LifeSIGNS to see how we could work together to promote their excellent work in mental health and in the hope that they would provide some useful literature and resources for our audiences. This was to be a project for the whole community.

Roll on rehearsals and an inspirational day workshop with Tim Ford, Artistic Director of the Lichfield Garrick and a few more visits from Mark and we had a production in super-fast fashion! With Self-Injury Awareness Day on March 1 we held our preview performances on 2-4 March 2016 and the play was extremely well received. Our presentation of the play was highly stylised and physical, with strong emphasis on the use of ensemble. We wanted it to be not only mentally stimulating but visually powerful too. The use of a large ensemble was a challenge but in a good, testing way! It allowed for lifts, imagery and choral speech which would not have been possible otherwise. The public audience reactions were even better than imagined:

Felt quite privileged watching tonight's performance really... cleverly put together and very moving.

Thank you for allowing me to see how exposed emotionally each and every one of you felt. I felt it as well... for all that the family have gone through, they survived it together with love.

I'm not one who gives theatrical praise out easily, but I thought it was really clever, really well acted and thoroughly enjoyable despite the subject matter. Best thing I've seen for a long time.

We also performed the play to all our Year 9 PSHE classes and their feedback too was impressive, with one teacher commenting:

The play's success lies in just how focused the students were. Mine can be a tricky group but they were really absorbed by your performance and commented so positively afterwards. In fact, they asked if they could go to more of these types of productions so, high praise from them! Certainly I feel a performance has the potential to convey a 'PSHE' style message far more powerfully than any other format.

Finally, we enjoyed some success performing in the Worcestershire Theatre Festival being nominated for 4 awards and claiming the silverware for Best Youth Actor. At the time of writing we look forward to performing in the Wallingford Festival, Oxfordshire. So drama teachers of the world, anything is possible with an idea and a little imagination...?!

All of us who have worked so hard in bringing 'Scratching the Surface' into being hope you enjoy this play but more than that, we hope you will gain an insight into the issue of self-harm as it becomes more prevalent in our society, particularly amongst young people. We hope this play helps you to have conversations with loved ones, friends or colleagues where before you might have shied away. We hope you will be better equipped to challenge misconceptions or better prepared to help someone in need should you find yourself in that situation.

Lastly we hope that if you are in this situation you understand there is support available whether at home, at school, through a charity or the NHS. You are not defined by this. There is hope. This dark time shall pass and there are healthier ways to manage how you are feeling. We hope that you too, like Rob, can look to the future and make plans; big, bright, amazing plans. "Next stop University?... Brilliant!"

Anna Allen
Head of Drama at Alderbrook School

Foreword by the playwright

It is always fabulous to have a compliment sent in your direction. This one was particularly appreciated following one of the performances of Scratching the Surface:

I brought my fledging GCSE year 9 group to one of the 'Scratching the Surface' previews. As always, Mark's theatrical style offered a unique, poignant & respectful treatment of a difficult subject. I wanted my students to understand the sort of theatre I love & support: ensemble, episodic, physical and true stories which speak to our human spirit. I was not disappointed. Keep up the great work...the type of British theatre which, I believe, is the most significant for all, regardless of age, gender, culture etc., yet is often not given enough attention. All involved with youth, family work or mental health should study Mark's plays as part of their training. Everyone could benefit from his amazing ability to encourage an audience to empathise in a society which is getting far too self-indulgent & egotistical.

Carly Sterne
Head of Drama, Lode Heath School

All plays begin in different ways. This one came my way, right out of the blue on 17 June 2015. So how does such a thing come about? Well... this is the edited highlights of the email I received:

Dear Mark,
Hello from Solihull and a fellow Drama teacher! I have so many questions and thoughts to email so I'm just going to jump straight in and hope that you can follow my drift! I have an idea... for you to write a play for a

young group of school aged actors - probably Year 9/10 and to enter the All England Theatre Festival for One Act plays 2016. I have never done this before. The thought both terrifies and excites me.
I asked the PSHE lead teacher at Alderbrook if she would like to 'commission' me to devise a play based on a theme of her choice.
She came back to me with the topic of self-harm and a Year 8/9 target audience believing that this is a key focus for young people, not only in Solihull but nationwide. According to the data, there has been a 20% increase in the number of 10 to 19 year old children admitted to hospital across the UK with self-harm injuries in the past few years.
As the hours went by, I started to think wider, in terms of our chosen audience. What if we
*were commissioned by someone (*ding* the local council, SMBC or a local charity perhaps) to create a hard-hitting, edgy play (possibly in partnership with a professional playwright or at least some workshop days with one) and we travelled into other secondary schools within the Borough? Would such a proposal be laughed at because there just isn't any money or would this help tick boxes on the Council's plan too? I have since contacted the Council, they are interested and I am awaiting further news.*
Obviously, it goes without saying I am a massive fan of your work; whilst looking on your website for a play about self-harm I noticed the tabs on consultancy / commissions, with a particular interest in groups wishing to create a one act play for a festival and... here we are.
I know you are ridiculously busy. I know a secondary school in south Solihull may have no interest to you at all. But if there is anything that sparks an interest in you from the above, please do get back in touch.

People, perhaps, imagine that I am somehow above being asked to write a play. Far from it. It was an absolute delight to receive the email. I wrote straight back.

'Scratching the Surface' has become the speediest piece of writing I have ever done (newfound benefits of being a full time playwright!). Anna was a complete superwoman and secured funding by mid-August! This unbelievable action gave me absolute confidence that I would be writing this piece for a dynamic drama teacher which, in turn, would mean well taught, self-assured and imaginative performers.

I interviewed the real people (provided by Anna) on the 8 October and sent an email with the full script attached on 25 November 2015. A week or so later I was watching the cast perform the opening section!

Self-harm is not a subject I would ever have chosen to write about. I'll be quite honest and say: I had little interest in it. I was taken aback by the passion with which the young people spoke about it and the concern they had for it. Consequently the play is as much about my ignorance being challenged as it is about self-harm. A key moment for me is the moment where one of the group suddenly said something which gave me a way of relating to the whole situation. Interestingly this moment was somewhat underplayed in the rehearsal I witnessed and I wanted to show my own relationship with the subject matter. I chose to include the interviews I did with the Drama group to expand on the information offered from Rob and his family's heartbreaking story. It is the fusion of the Drama group and Rob's story which offers real opportunities for imaginative staging which I really enjoy seeing and is key to the presentation of my plays. I don't want the play to have any one way of being performed. This really will have to be interpreted differently by anyone looking to produce it.

Anna's group at Alderbrook exemplified this approach. They used a variety of approaches and even, at one point staged a scene (without changing any of the words) as a game show! It was this level of daring that I most appreciated in the production. As I said to them, what interests me when I go to see a play of mine is not what I have written. I like to see things I hadn't even thought of in the interpretation.

Thanks Anna and Alderbrook cast; I couldn't have asked for more from you all and in record time. I was watching it as part of the AETF in March 2016 (just 4 months after starting the writing process i.e. interviews).

I hope it has made you think that perhaps it is worth contacting me if you are considering offering me a commission. Nine times out of ten I will be flattered and enthusiastic.

Mark Wheeller

The DVD of the original Alderbrook production
is available from Mark Wheeller.

See page 61 for further details.

Scratching the Surface

Cast
Rob
Mark
Louise
Jim
Ollie
Sandy

The Ensemble
This can be flexible in number. In this version of the script I have included Girls and Boys 1-3.

For the original Alderbrook production:

Rob: Tom Marriott
Mark: David Thompson
Louise: Jess Thompson
Jim: Oliver Moore
Ollie: George Bowen
Sandy: Georgia Sheward

The Ensemble:

Hasan Ali	Beatrice Castle
Erica Goldman	Harry Griffiths
James Hunter	Hannah Lockhart
Evie Middlemiss	Steven Mullen
Zainamb Panwar	Max Petts

Director: Anna Allen
Stage Manager: John Fennell
Dep. Stage Manager: Louisa Halliwell-Ewen
Original Musical Underscore: John Fennell

Section 1: Introducing... and an end?

A movement scene with a modern guitar based underscore is performed by the ensemble to represent the emotional process of those who self-harm using the following stages:

1	*The seed – Isolated and lost*
2	*The secret – Trapped and attacked*
3	*The exposure – Naked and vulnerable*
4	*The help – Relief and escape*
5	*The regret - Conflict and pain*

The ensemble move aside leaving Rob on the floor, centre stage, alone.

Sandy: (*Sandy enters with Mark. Indicating*) This is Rob. Rob, this is Mark.

Rob: *(Getting up slightly embarrassed)* Hello.

Sandy: Where do you want to sit Rob?

Mark: He'll be fine there. I'm recording on this (*iPhone*) and also on this other device, *(portable cassette player).* This relic is called a cassette player and it's already recording!
I guess you've never done anything like this before. (*Rob shakes his head.)*
So, who talked you into doing this?

Rob: Mum.

Mark: Oh right.

Mark: How come you were willing to be involved?

Rob: Dunno.

Section 1

(Silence)

Mark: There has to be a reason.

Rob: Same as mum? (*Indicates Louise*)

Mark: Explain?

Rob: To help people I guess.

Mark: Louise?

Louise: Apart from living through it, I have to go to a meeting twice a day at work, where we talk about patients. I'm a nurse. The children and adolescents with mental health issues are always flagged up so we always know why they've been admitted. It's <u>often</u> for self-harm.

G1: Trying to find relief.

Louise: DSH.

G2: Trying to make myself feel more human.

Louise: Deliberate Self Harm.

B1: Trying to release pain.

B2: To relieve pain.

Louise: It goes in fits and starts. It tails off through the summer, picks back up again after and climaxes at exam time.

B3: Trying to get rid of one pain by making it another.

Louise: Whilst it was the elephant in the room for us, I don't want it to be like that for anyone else.

B2: Or the mouse in the room.

Mark: (*Turns to B2*) Explain?

B2: You feel like a small helpless being, to the point that you'd hurt yourself and, like everyone around is different to you.

Rob: I almost didn't come.

Mark: *(Turning back to Rob)* Really?

Rob: Yeh.

Jim: I didn't expect him to turn up! It's not uncommon for... you can arrange something for Rob,
"Yeh, ok I'll go."
... and he just won't turn up!

Louise: I was delighted he'd arrived safely.

Rob: I <u>was</u> late.

Jim: But, you arrived. I'd been waiting for phone calls saying "Go home! And take him to the meeting!"

Mark: I hope you've not been worrying about it.

Section 1

Louise: His biggest fear was:

Rob: How do I get through the gate?

Louise: ... and...

Rob: What's he gonna ask me?

Mark: I'll just want you to tell me things that you think I ought to know to... to make a... a play about this subject. I've also spoken to a Drama group... I was shocked to discover how many had experience of self-harm... second-hand... and in some cases first-hand:

B1: When I've done it, it's been through anger. I've had four... three family members with depression and friends with depression.
(*Long pause for thought... welling up*)
I was angry at myself that I couldn't do anything to help them. So (*sniffs trying to hold back tears*) I wanted to take my anger out on something and I... (*breaking down*)... I felt like it needed to be taken out on me...

Mark: Am I allowed to ask what you did, or not?

B1: I used to...

Mark: Stop, if you want. I sense you want to carry on...

B1: Yeh, yeh. I punch glass. I dip my head under the water in the bath. I... (*crying*) I cut myself. I do anything to make myself feel... to just take the anger away. I... anything that could make me hurt the way I thought they were feeling. It sounds stupid but, I used to ride on my bike and just wouldn't stop... just pedal until my legs started burning to make me feel more human... like, as if I could do something.

Rob: I might not be very eloquent.

Mark: That's fine, that's fine.

B2: My friends... you wouldn't get any of this information out of them but with a group of people that do, like drama and that sort of ... we're more open...

G2: I'd just make the shower water too hot or anything like that so... no one would ever find out. Just be like scratching your hand down a brick wall or something.
I know a lot of people did it for attention. That upsets me because it takes the attention away from those that really need it.

B3: It's like the boy who cried wolf.

G1: A lot of people who do it for attention, kind of, do it in really obvious places so people can see it and...

G2: They post it on Instagram, then you get comments saying
"I'm here for you"
... and things... but a true self-harmer wouldn't want anyone to find out, you know.

Section 1

Rob: I don't think they should say "true self-harmer". Some people do it for attention but because they need help, if that makes sense?

Mark: Yeh, okay.
We'll also hear from your mum, dad and Ollie, your brother as well... in the play it'll seem like they're here (*Jim Louise & Ollie wave*), like the Drama group, (*everyone else waves*) but obviously they're not.
I told Rob a bit about me... but shan't bore you with that... apart from this:
(To Rob) The words you all say to me will become like a big jigsaw puzzle for me to piece together. So it will be real words... exclusively!
Then I launched into the interview...
Are you happy to start talking or do you want to...

Rob: ... yeh but give me, like a prompt?

Mark: (*Smiling)* Of course. Well, let's start with the ending... is there an ending?

Louise: I think that's up to Rob...

Rob: It'll always be there. I might not do it for years like, but I could always relapse. It'll stay with me forever. It changed my life.

Louise: For me a positive sign for the future was him going Tanzania.
He came home one day in Year 11 and said:

Rob: We need to go to this evening at school.

Louise: I remember sitting in the hall listening to this guy from the company thinking:
"Shit, he might not be allowed to go."
We had to declare everything.

Rob: We all had to raise four and a half grand each, bag packs in supermarkets, table-top sales, a sponsored abseil off a bridge... though it wasn't hard… wasn't very high.

Louise: He had to fit in, to, er, to be a team player, take initiative and not be spoon-fed. He ended up being one of the key players, a leader.

Rob: I don't think so.

Jim: You used your scouting experience, showing people how to put tents up and…

Rob: That's not really leadership.

Jim: … what to do… ?

Mark: Mentoring?

Jim: Yes.

Rob: I just showed them what to do.

Jim: That's leading!

Rob: I just do what's necessary.

Mark: So, for you, it wasn't anything special but other people perceived it as something a bit different?

Section 1

Rob: Seems that way.

Mark: What happened there?

Rob: A week of acclimatization, then went to a National Park looking at wildlife, getting used to the weather, then a week of projects, we built... what did we build? We built, like a school sort of thing. Then a week of walking, then a week of rest and relaxation in like a... in Zanzibar just sitting on the beach.

Louise: It transformed him into a different person. He can now talk about things.

Mark: So, there is a positive end to this?

Jim: I don't think it will end for us.

Mark: Go on.

Jim: There'll always be something won't there?

Louise: I liken it to the children I work with who have cancer. Once you have that diagnosis, irrespective of how long you are out of your cure stage, it sits on your shoulder. I guess that's what you're trying to say.

Rob: I don't think Tanzania turned it round. I just think it sort of, just stopped. I... just didn't feel the need to do it.

Louise: Some of the reason why it stopped was because you were pissed off with going to see that psychiatrist!

Rob: She was shit though! (*Laughter*)

Mark: Next stop University?

Rob: Yeh. Physics at Swansea is my first choice. Kent is my reserve.

Mark: Brilliant!

Section 2: An Angry Child

Mark: So, tell me anything about your childhood up until the point that...

Louise: Rob was born on 3 September 1996, weighing 9lb 3oz. A perfect, healthy newborn baby boy. 10 fingers and 10 little toes. We became a family. He was a dreadful sleeper and would often need to be occupied.

Jim: As he grew, he was big and strong, and had lots of energy. He had tantrums, like all toddlers.

Louise: By the time he was 3 he was excellent at completing jigsaws. *(Pause)* He did have tantrums but mainly when he was with others.

Rob: I was a bit of an angry child I guess. I was kicked out of Nursery.

Mark: Because?

Rob: Chucked a chair at a teacher.

Mark: Why?

Rob: Don't remember. Erm... I'm not very good at this, sorry...

Mark: No worries. You've never talked about it before so it's like, you're processing it, as you speak.

Louise: He'd be often in trouble at school and it was that, that alerted us to think that maybe... maybe we needed a bit more help with him... people kept saying:

Ensemble: But he's just so intelligent!

Louise: Writing was a problem but he was an avid reader so there was a disconnect there.

Jim: He was naughty though.

Louise: Yeh, really struggled in group situations…

Rob: *(Justifying)* Didn't like sharing.

Louise: Hated sharing… hated playing anything by the rules. So, if you're playing Monopoly, he'd just throw it up in the air…

Rob: Monopoly's pathetic!

Louise: His language was "flowery"…from probably… nine-ish, I'd say.
He hated anything that would draw attention to himself. Drama, the end of term play, Christmas nativity. He'd be disruptive to be withdrawn from it.

Mark: What kind of things did you do?

Rob: Can't remember.

Mark: Oh please!

Rob: I don't know. When was this?

Louise: Always actually!

Jim: … just messed around in general.

Section 2

Louise: Make loud noises, run across the stage and... I distinctly remember a... at er... Year 3. Everyone was attentive but Rob was there counting the ceiling tiles!

Rob: I wanted to know how many green ones there were!

Mark: (*Laughing*) So, are you gonna disagree with your mum and say "I loved Drama... it was the best thing ever."?

Rob: No. It's fucking shit! (*Laughter*)

Louise: His enquiring mind was a distraction.
My dad was one of his carers while I was at work and would take him to the Science Museum, so science was driven into you from a very early age. Jim was doing a lot of property maintenance around our house, so there'd be tools around, and he'd show Rob how to use them...

Jim: *(laughing)*... with disastrous results!

Louise: He had support throughout junior school with behaviour but we started to dig a bit deeper particularly pending the move to secondary school and then educational psychologists' became involved.

Sandy: I think Rob's mum was behind looking more deeply into things Rob was finding difficult. She just wanted him to be statemented.

Mark: (*Introducing*) Sandy… the Special Needs Co-ordinator at Rob's secondary school, who was with Rob for his interview with me.

Sandy: You were assessed to death, weren't you?

Rob: I refused to get out of the car at first. Kicked and screamed and… I was only 8 or 9. I was a little shit!

Louise: We'd have friends over and… and Rob would kick off. I remember he'd done something and was taken up to his room. We were in the garden and he just threw things out of the window. (*Rob sniggers*) It became difficult for us to socialise as a family cos he wasn't having any of it. We went to this same friend's house and he broke something in one of their girls rooms…

Ollie: They had, erm, something dangling down over the bed, like, beads hanging down over the bed?

Louise: … and he broke them, but denied all knowledge of it. It was difficult, type of thing, to put people in that situation.
In 2007 he was diagnosed with Asperger's. I remember the consultant psychologist…

(Lines labelled G/B throughout the play should be delivered by any ensemble member representing the relevant character)

G/B He's the same boy as when you came into the room ten minutes ago. Nothing's changed.

Section 2

Louise:	But for us, everything had changed. We never challenged the diagnosis but they did say:
G/B	This was a multi-professional decision but we really struggled with this case.
Jim:	Junior School were giving up on him, saying
G/B	Have a word with him or we'll have to do something.
Louise:	You were excluded quite...
Rob:	Once!
Louise:	From Junior School?
Rob:	*(Assertively)* I was excluded once.
Louise:	Yeh. Okay.
Rob:	I used to hide under the desks at school.
Mark:	What reaction did you get?
Rob:	Wasn't seeking a reaction.
Mark:	Right.
Rob:	Everyone was just like:
G/B	Oh yeah, it's Rob being weird!
Mark:	Would they say that or would you...?
Rob:	Just feel it.

Mark: Why didn't you do this kind of thing at home?

Rob: There were no desks to hide under!
I used to bang my head... but that...

Mark: So in what kind of situation would that happen?

Rob: Arguments between mum and dad. Like, normal arguments everyone has... but it seemed worse if you get what I mean.

Mark: But you weren't involved in these arguments?

Rob: I was like:
"Stop arguing!"

Jim: We're not arguing!

Rob: "You are!"
Then it turned into me and them arguing... yeh.

Mark: Okay. And how hard do you bang your head... did it bleed?

Rob: Nothing like that!

Mark: So, kind of gentle banging your head.

Rob: Sort of, yeh.

Mark: Were they concerned?

Rob: Dunno.

Mark: What do you reckon?

Section 2

Rob:	Mum used to yell at me when I did it.
Mark:	Did that stop you?
Rob:	Not really.
Mark:	Did it make it worse?
Rob:	I guess. Like, I can't really remember much cos it's ages ago.
Mark:	So... self-harm is more than about cutting. It can be hitting walls?
B2:	In my mind that's like a similar but a different cos I punch a wall quite regularly... probably about four, five times a week I'll punch a wall I don't think of that as self-harm.
Mark:	Well, you are harming yourself aren't you? I've never thought of it like that before either, but I reckon it is.
B2:	I don't punch the wall to hurt myself.
G2:	I think it depends on the intent.
B2:	It would be that I'm that angry at something... normally with work... it's either that I punch the wall or I punch someone, so it's the wall that gets it. I'm... I'm releasing my anger by punching that wall.
Mark:	But I think by widening the definition like you've done, helps me, as someone who has never done it, to understand why someone

might do it because it's essentially the same thing. Do you get what I'm saying?

B2: Yeh, but I think...

Mark: And if you do it repeatedly there's no difference. It's just a wall or blade...

B2: I suppose but like I said... like, when I punch a wall or whatever it... maybe I punch a steering wheel or whatever but I'm not trying to hurt my hand...

Mark: What you've said has suddenly given me a way of being able to understand and relate to it cos I can understand that sense of frustration where you want to take it out on something so suddenly I can relate to it and, I'll be honest... I haven't until this moment.

Rob: There were nice things that happened. It wasn't all shit. Skiing, I've been skiing since I could walk... holidays. That was fun.

Sandy: Rob's quite outdoorsy.

Rob: Mum and Dad were always very like

Jim & Louise: Stop watching TV and go outside and play.

Sandy: He does scouts.

Rob: Done it since beavers... scout leader now, in charge of kids.

Section 2

Mark: You're a big fan of Scouts?

Rob: Yeh. If you do it, you know it's good. If you don't, you think it's all about knots!

Ollie: One memory I have from junior school was; I was playing football and someone shouted:

G/B: I'm a murderer!

Ollie: It was Rob.

Rob: What???

Ollie: You'd cut up a worm. You were digging a hole and you chopped it up!

G/B I'm a murderer!

Ollie: No idea why I remember it but I do!

Rob: Probably joking.

Louise: We were we were really worried about the transition from Junior to Secondary because those with Asperger's struggle with change. It was from a three hundred school to over a thousand.

Mark: And this is where you come in?

Sandy: I met him in Year 6 to help with his transition as he was statemented so I saw him on a one to one basis.

Rob: I wasn't communicating properly or something wasn't it? I don't know how to describe it...

Sandy: Yeh.

Mark: Doing this must be like super hard then? How are you feeling inside?

Rob: Shit.

Mark: Sorry?

Rob: Normally it's not something you talk about but if it helps someone else... just, you know, so you're not alone and stuff.

Louise: The bizarre thing about this for me is that ever since it... it started, it's been the elephant in the room, so actually him talking about it... is amazing cos... well, I'm not confident he ever talked to the professionals.

Section 3 – The Elephant in the Room

Mark: What did you know about self-harm?

B1: Not much.

Mark: Do you know anybody who's done it?

B1: Yes.

Mark: You do?

B1: Yes. Like two or three.

Mark: What do you know and what you think about it?

B1: Just cut themselves cos they was depressed but like, it didn't help cos they just got more depressed.

G1: What I've learnt is that some people do it for real and some people do it for attention and people who do it for attention probably don't suffer from depression. I've known a few people who do suffer from depression and they don't want to show it at all. They're very secretive about it.

G3: When you start to hurt yourself it's difficult to stop cos you feel like you're taking out your sadness on yourself. Most people have a load of sadness within them so they don't stop until they've got the sadness out. Some people can't get the sadness out so it's difficult to get out of that cycle. It can follow you and stab you in the back sometimes.

G1 There's been a thing on the internet about One Direction and Justin Bieber… getting people… younger girls to "cut for them". They were posting pictures on the internet of like…

Mark: Oh to prove….

G1: … to prove that they love them and…

B3: I think it started off as like an internet joke yeah…

Mark: But did people actually do it?

G1: Yeh, I'm not on Facebook but my friend showed me pictures and it was #cutforzayne. I was thinking to myself why would you want to do that? It… it's not important… when there's… why would you want to cause such a big fuss about someone leaving a band?

Mark: So Rob, erm, tell me about the self-harm. The thing I imagine is, like grazes on your arm?

Rob: It's more than grazes, right. I've still got scars from two years ago.

Mark: Just arms?

Rob: Wherever it's easiest to hide. Thighs.

Mark: Do you still do it?

Rob: Not really.

Section 3

Mark: How long ago did you stop?

Rob: Two years ago. But you sometimes still get the urge. It's addictive... like... it relaxes you n stuff. You feel in control I guess.

Mark: Had you seen someone else doing it?

Rob: No.

Mark: So, it wasn't, like, a copycat thing?

Rob: Not that I can remember, no.

Mark: What age were you?

Rob: Year 9. Thirteen. Er... I was into making models and they all came with a pack of blades.

Mark: How does a situation brew, that leads you to...

Rob: There's a build up over a period of weeks and I... the idea would flash into my head and I'd just, sort of, suppress it and then...

Mark: How would the idea form itself?

Rob: Erm. I don't know. Erm.
(*Silence*)
It's just there at the back your mind, after arguing or something.
(*After a pause for thought*) It's like an itch on your arm... I don't know how to describe it...

Mark: That's a great description!

Rob: I always knew it was a bit stupid but it didn't seem like there was any other way at the time.
Once you do it, it affects your life in a big way.

Sandy: That was an issue in PE. I got you permission to wear a rugby shirt at one point.

Rob: Yeh, you have to hide it and stuff. Even now, I still sort of keep my arm close to my body when I get changed. It's become a natural thing to do.

Mark: Yet today, you're wearing a tee shirt.

Rob: Yeh. It's alright now. Cos, yeh.

Mark: *(To Rob)* Does it hurt when you do it?

Rob: (*Nonchalantly*) You sort of get numb to it.

Mark: So, it's not nice?

Rob: Dunno. It's complicated.

Louise: Initially we assumed it was a copy-cat thing, probably cos we struggled to relate to it, erm, and the friendships that he had at that time, for want of a better word, they were a bit... grungie, gothic looking.

Jim: Some of them were a bit strange looking weren't they?

Section 3

Rob: *(Quietly outraged)* No!

Louise: Some are still his friends... be careful Jim, be careful.

Mark: Were you a bit grungie or gothy?

Louise: He'd have been in black and his hair was longer.

Rob: That's cos I didn't like getting it cut!

Louise: His music was all heavy metal and...

Mark: What kind of bands?

Rob: Erm, Metallica. Nothing too bad. (*Louise bristles. To Louise*) Well it was bad to you!

Louise: Slipknot?

Rob: Slipknot? I didn't really listen to them! You just heard it once and thought "Oh my god!" "Oh no!"

Louise: *(Laughing)* For me, the heavier the music, coming out of his room, the more we were losing him.

Rob: You're talking out of your arse! (*To Mark*) I just liked the music.

Mark: And it didn't reflect your mood?

Rob: I listen to sadder music now.

Louise: *(Disapproving)* Yeh that blues stuff!

Rob: God! (*Laughter*)

(*Silence*)

Mark: Do you remember the first time your mum discovered the cuts?

Rob: I didn't know how much she'd care really... nor how much effort it'd be to hide it. I'd just gone to bed like normal...

Mark: Yeh.

Rob: I put a tee-shirt on and went to sleep and... maybe my arm flopped out and I just woke up and mum saw it...

Louise: No Rob. It wasn't like that.
It was brought to our attention actually by your school. But, before that I remember, it was erm... it was er... er... springtime...

Rob: *(Sarcastic)* Birds were tweeting!

Louise: He'd started sleeping in a sweat shirt and... and... I remember saying to him in the hallway:
"Bloody hell Rob, you're not self-harming and covering up are you?"
... completely flippant, never, for one minute, thinking I'd hit the nail on the head!
He just kind of... rolled his eyes, didn't deny it, you know, we were rushing out and I didn't think any more about it.
Shortly after this, I was hanging washing out in the

garden… another beautiful day (*Rob makes bird noises*) and then his deputy head phoned.

G/B: I've been alerted to the fact that Robert may be self-harming.

Louise: I was quite defensive. I remember saying:
"Is it not a stage? The friends he's hanging around with… they're all, you know… "
When I put the phone down the world completely fell apart. (*Breaks down*) I rang a friend, erm, her daughter was a year older than Rob. She pulled up Rob's Facebook and said:

G/B: They're all doing it.

Louise: There were these, er, quotes. When I googled them, they were words out of songs, but very symbolic for me.
Then I realised…
"Shit! My mum and dad are coming! What the hell am I gonna do?"
It needed to be fixed before I told them, but I… I rang my dad in tears and told them:

G/B: Are you sure?

Louise: I don't know. The school told us.

G/B: Where is he now?

Louise: He's out… I don't know what he's doing. He could be…

G/B: Let him come back with us for the weekend.

Louise: No. I need... we need to decide what to do. Look, I may see you later but if I'm consumed by this, you know, I might not.

G/B: Why don't you come for something to eat Lou?

Louise: They took me out to the pub purely just to get me out.
I remember picking Ollie up on my way back. He would have known I was upset. When we pulled up onto our drive I saw Rob coming out of the house with his friends... (*whispers*)... grungy friends (*laughs*)... I was thinking:
"Oh my God! Where's he going? Is he going to hang himself?"

Rob: This is ridiculous!

Louise: To me, there was nothing in between.
I went into the house, terribly upset and I thought "I need to get him to the doctors!"
I got an emergency appointment and sat in the blooming waiting room just sobbing with the (*laughing*) blooming receptionist just watching me. Other people were around, you know, just pretending I'm not there.
The doctor took it very, very seriously and said she'd contact the Child and Adolescent Mental Health Services, CAHMS, and that they'd contact us later that day.

Mark: You still hadn't talked to Rob about it?

Section 3

Louise:	No. I was scared I'd push him into doing... something even more erm... The doctor came back and said:
G/B:	We'll do a multi-professional team meeting in the morning to discuss it and then we'll come back to you.
Louise	I remember telling Jim and... I don't know if you remember...
Jim:	No.
Louise:	Rob's cutting himself.
Jim:	How do you know?
Louise:	The school contacted me.
Jim:	They must have got it wrong!
Louise:	Jim, he's definitely doing it. I remember going into his room late that night when he was asleep, pulling up his sleeve and you could see... he was in a sweatshirt and you could... you could see the cuts.
Mark:	Weren't you worried he might wake up?
Louise:	He's a very heavy sleeper.
Jim:	*(Laughing)* Very, very heavy sleeper.
Mark:	Did you see multiple wounds?

Louise: Yes, yes.

Jim: Like, scratch marks on his arm

Louise: About ten I'd say. Ten.

Jim: That's right.

Mark: And were they red or were they healed or... ?

Louise: Erm... no... yes... both. Yeh.

Jim: I kept checking, going into his room constantly to see he's ok. Still do it now don't we?

Mark: So, it's affected, I guess, everything about your father-son relationship?

Jim: Mmm. *(Long pause)*

Louise: I remember thinking:
"I've got to move everything that, you know... he might... you know... ropes" (*Rob gives Louise a "look"*) Don't look at me like...

Rob: What ropes do we have in the house?

Louise: I know I was being irrational but... string, whatever.

Rob: String?

Louise: I'd find blades in all sorts of places and think:
"Oh I missed that!"

A few weeks later I thought...
"Pencil sharpeners?"
I found them with no blades and thought:
"Too late for that then?"
I was still trying to tell myself "this was just a phase" and "they're all doing it" but something was...I went into this awful panic. ... and I started to hide tablets and...
The next morning the doctor got back to me wanting Rob that afternoon for an appointment. I still hadn't spoken to him. I thought, if I could get him to speak to a doctor, of some description, everything would be OK, but you wouldn't bloody come would you?

Rob: Nope.

Louise: I remember saying... trying to s... be calm. I knew from history, it was better just to... with no warning rather than have big, you know, worry about it... so:
"Rob, I need to take you to the doctors."

Rob: You weren't calm. You were yelling and I was – "Why are you yelling at me?

Louise: We need to go to the doctors. You've got to come! This is ridiculous. You need help! You're ill! You've got to bloody come!

Rob: I'm not going!

Louise: You're really ill!

Rob: I was sitting in bed. I remember her shouting:

Louise: We've got to go... we've got to go now!

Rob: Then she started to cry.
"Why are you crying?"

Louise: All he could say was:

Rob: I'm not going.

Louise: Then just turning over and shouting:

Rob: Get out!

Louise: So I did. I didn't know what else to do.
I rang the clinic and said:
"I can't get him to come. I'm so sorry. Can someone come out? He really needs help."

G/B I'm afraid not, but if you get him here before five, we will see him.

Louise: He'd put things in front of his door so I couldn't get in. He didn't come out for food.

Rob: I just remember mum screaming and going mental.

Louise: I was quite mental!

Mark: Did the doctor come eventually?

Louise: No.

Section 3

Mark:	I'm shocked.
Louise:	So was I. What they've since said is, if you're in that position, call 999 but if he didn't want to go, there's no way an ambulance man would have got him there.
Mark:	So, when Jim came home from work you presumably said: "I haven't managed to get Rob to the hospital?" How did that conversation go? I can imagine me being: "Why didn't you get him there? Why didn't you phone me?"
Louise:	Erm... I think it... you, to me, you did the right thing. You just gave me a hug.
Mark:	Ah.
Ollie:	That's cute.
Jim:	There was no point me going upstairs trying to make him go. That would have made it worse, but we knew he had to go at some stage.
Mark:	So, did all this make you want to do it more or... ??
Rob:	Probably cos I was stressed out. Sometimes it feels like you deserve it because... I don't know how... you know... I don't...
Louise:	I was almost condoning it, you know, helping out. I'd got long-sleeved tops to wear underneath cos

you could see cuts through his shirt. I'm thinking "this is ridiculous... absolutely ridiculous!", but, as a mum, you're supposed to help and support. The buying of long sleeves went on for months.
For our summer holiday, we went to Greece. It was hot. Rob wore long-sleeved vests if he came out, but actually he spent most of the time inside on his own.

Rob: Reading... reading! I wasn't just sitting there!

Ollie: There were arguments every day to get him to come out.

Louise: When we were asleep, I recall him walking round the room. I was convinced he was looking for something to cut himself with. I didn't challenge him for fear of pushing him into an acute situation in a foreign country with no support.

Mark: So how did you move it forward to get these professionals involved?

Louise: Three or four months down the line. Erm... actually, a little bit of me was like, "I don't blame you for not wanting to go", because, it'd been hard when he was having some of the investigations for the Asperger's, and we hadn't seen any positive result.
He got on really well with the paediatrician he was seeing for his ADHD, and I called her for help as he was refusing to see CAMHS. We "manufactured" an appointment and she insisted on taking Rob's

	blood pressure on the "cut" arm without me in the room. She asked him what he had done to his arm.
Rob:	Fell out of a tree.
Louise:	She challenged him but he still kept up the pretence.
Ollie:	I remember going to the hospital and sitting outside the door while you and Rob were in there. I still didn't know anything.
Mark:	Were there tensions between the two of you?
Ollie:	Yeh.
Mark:	Over what kind of thing?
Rob:	Him being a twat.
Jim:	Anything.
Mark:	Give me an example.
Jim:	Ollie could be wearing the wrong deodorant, brushing his hair back.
Rob:	Oh shut up? Wearing the wrong deodorant? What're you on about?
Mark:	So Rob, you give me an example...
Rob:	Doing something stupid and pissing me off!

Ollie: There'd've been arguments over X-Box. Say I'm on it and Rob wanted a go....

Rob: You were always on it!

Jim: *(Laughing)* It belonged to him!!!

Rob: Mum you're all lovey dovey with your sister. You'd be going:
"Oh my God this is so different. It's so shit!
They're gonna hate each other!"
We were just normal.

Mark: Do you see it as normal or not?

Ollie: Erm, yeh, I'd say so. We were a normal family who just argued a bit.

Mark: When did you find out about Rob self-harming?

Louise: When Rob was in Year 10.

Ollie: I had a paper round. Mum helped with it.

Rob: You never did it!

Ollie: Don't say that!

Jim: You didn't do yours either so you can't bloody talk!

Ollie: We'd parked up by the bank to deliver them and mum just started breaking down.
"What's up?"

Section 3

Louise: I'm going to tell you something that will shock you Ollie, but I think you need to know. Rob's been self-harming.

Mark: How did he react?

Louise: There weren't many words... just lots of hugs...

Ollie: Yeh.

Louise: ... and tears.

Ollie: Then we went and did the papers!

Mark: How did it affect your relationship with Rob?

Ollie: Erm... I just tried to carry on as normal really and...

Mark: So, was it the elephant in the room again?

Ollie: Yeh. Always.

Louise: Throughout this time I'd ring Ollie, if I couldn't get hold of Rob.

Ollie: Once, she asked me to check if he was still breathing.

Louise: That was after Rob's GCSE physics exam. He'd texted me at work... just...
"That's it. Shit."
Alarm bells rang and I felt panicked. In my head he was in a school toilet cutting himself. I was in a real state but knew I wouldn't be able to search

through school for him.
I rang Sandy, who rang back within half an hour saying:

Sandy: He was disappointed but he's ok.

Louise: I translated that to "at least he's alive".
Later I rang Ollie:
"Rob's exam hasn't gone well, I'm worried. Please check on him."
I was waiting for the screaming as I thought he'd be swinging from the rafters.

Ollie: He's fine. Don't worry.

Louise: That evening I made fajitas and nachos. I'd often resort to food as being a "pick-him-up" kind of medicine.

Ollie: I never thought he'd do anything ridiculously severe. I was more worried about mum and how she'd react.

Louise: There was a time things weren't going well for Ollie at school. He had his Swiss army knife and I asked
"What are you doing with that?"

Ollie: I was thinking of cutting myself.

Louise: Ollie, I can't go through this again.

Ollie: Sorry mum... I...

Section 3

Louise: We both cried.
It's shaped our relationship. He looks out for me. Only this week I noticed blood on his cuff. I spent a couple of hours worrying until he provided a logical explanation. The fact he came home in a jumper initially confirmed my suspicion despite it being a cold, autumnal day.

Rob: That is ridiculous!

Louise: It might well be but no parent would be any different. A number of times, I'd drive home cos, in my head, Rob's swinging from the rafters.

Mark: Have you ever thought of suicide?

Rob: Yeh. Couple of times.

Mark: Really?

Rob: Yeh.

Mark: Can you tell me about those thoughts? Or would you rather not?

Rob: Dunno. Erm…

Mark: Fair enough… Rob didn't want to elaborate… but… and this is the absolute truth… one lad from the theatre group I spoke to suddenly said, with no real warning…

B1: I've had one family member die because of depression… and self-harm.

Mark: Suicide?

B1: Yeh, they couldn't cope. Then I've also had someone who's shown me that if you speak to someone you can get through. I've got a very, very close friend who self-harms and I just felt, like, everything built up inside and I just needed to release it. So… I broke one of the razors *(long pause to gather thoughts and hold back emotions)* I went down the bottom of the garden… *(long pause, blows nose)*… and I kind of felt better.

Section 4

Mark: They were being incredibly open. I said:
"I wasn't expecting any of this. I... I'm really amazed that this is something that you all seem to relate to so closely."

So, where did you cut yourself?

B1: Like... on my side and my leg. It made me feel better and then the next day I just felt really bad again.

Mark: I'm really sorry to keep asking questions...

B1: It's alright.

Mark: ... but how did it make you feel better and for how long?

B1: I was shaking when I did it. It just helped me cos now I know what they'd gone through and I needed to try harder with them.

Mark: How long ago was this?

B1: About a year ago.

Mark: So where are you now and is this ever...

B1: Never gonna happen again.

Mark: It's never gonna happen again?

B1: No, no.

Mark: You say that very definitely.

B1: Yeh.

Mark: Because?

B1: It took me to a really bad place.

Mark: Right.

B1: It'll never happen again.

Mark: How did you get out of that really bad place?

B1: I spoke to my mum.

Mark: Brave.

B1: I just said:
"Mum, I don't feel right."
And then she spoke to me and I spoke to my girlfriend and it helped.

B3: People who self-harm feel like there is no one they can speak to. Speaking to or even listening to someone who's done it is more likely to help you get you over it.

Section 5: Loneliness and goodnight kisses

Sandy: In Year 10, I was working with you, one to one, and you said...
"I'm feeling shit."

Rob: Did I?

Sandy: You'd been Googling?

Rob: Had I? *(Looks up obviously concerned)*

Mark: Do you want me to stop recording?

Rob: No. It's alright?

Sandy: Did you remember talking to me about bi-polar?

Rob: No.

Sandy: You'd been Googling...

Rob: Had I?

Sandy: Yeh.

(*Silence*)

Mark: Had you come across this before or was this the first time?

Sandy: Only with girls but at that time it was linked to a Hollyoaks story. That was the first time I came across it.

Mark: Ahhhhhh! Right.

Sandy: Somebody had done it and then friends had copied so, completely different circumstances to Rob's.

Rob: If I found out someone else was doing it I always wonder if I've fucked up, that they'd seen and copied me.

Mark: Has that happened?

Rob: Don't think so.

Mark: Right. *(Pause)* So, what led you do this?

Rob: Stressed with school and stuff...

Mark: Exams?

Rob: Yeh.

Mark: Relationships?

Rob: Not really... just... everyone was, like, this is really important. You've got to do well. You've got to do it. You've got to do it. You've got to do it... but it wasn't just because of exams. I think everyone gets stressed but deals with it in different ways.

Mark: So, did your way of dealing with it, deal with it?

Rob: For me it was never really a conscious thing, like I said about the itch like, it's just sort of happens...

Mark: ... and instinctively you scratch it?

Section 5

Rob: Yeh.

Mark: Yeh. And this would happen at home?

Rob: Yeh.

Mark: Never in school?

Rob: (*Thoughtfully*) Yeh.

Mark: With what?

Rob: A lighter.

Mark Lighting your arm?

Rob: No. Heated the metal bit around the edge and did it that way.

Mark: And that must have left a shape rather than a cut?

Rob: Yeh.

Louise: One of the things that I see and makes this so compelling really, is the huge number of kids that are in crisis, harming themselves in some way and are admitted to a hospital.

Mark: So, Ollie, in Year 11... what number would you say do this?

Ollie: Above fifty percent I'd say...

Mark: You're joking!

Ollie: Mostly girls.

Mark: So of that 50% what percentage would be boys and what percentage would be girls?

Ollie: Erm... ten ninety or maybe less.

Jim: Doing it regularly or just one off?

Ollie: Enough to be able to tell.

Mark: Why are they doing it?

Ollie: Some for attention, but others... I don't know.

Mark: Why?

Rob: Talking about it maybe.

Ollie: I'd say it's social media. You hear more about it.

Louise: For me, the reason as to why he was doing it, faded into complete insignificance. We just needed to stop it. I didn't care why it was happening. If you're unwell, you're given a pill and you get better. I was searching for the pill... not the reason why you might have got the illness... you know.

Mark: Do you think that's the right way round?

Louise: It was the way we were able to function in our lives.

Mark: Is there anything anyone else wants...

B2: We are a generation that wants to be liked. When you see that "like" on your photo you think "Oh my God I'm, I'm being liked", but there's all this negative energy as well. So just as easily you can feel you're nothing... not worth being here almost... not loved and alone in the world. That's hard.

B1: I'm glad to be tackling this head on because, most of the time, the person doing the self-harm isn't the reason for the self-harm. Sometimes its people being demoralising or mean to them... like from family, or peers. Sometimes it's bullying. Whatever the reason it needs tackling.

Mark: Well, I'll just finish off by saying that this experience of talking to you has been remarkable for me. I had no idea there was this kind of... erm... passion behind this topic.

Louise: One thing more... I just... not particular words but I remember actions. There were two nights when we didn't have the "Goodnight, I love you." ... and a hug from Rob. Those were the two nights directly after the school phoning and the contact with CAHMS. That's probably really trivial but it was really profound for me.

Mark: Well, I hope you get a goodnight kiss tonight.

Rob: Erm... maybe... you asked about why I did it... well... maybe... maybe I felt lonely as well. Just... dunno. Even though I had friends, it's a lot of effort to maintain friendships.

I did want to put the effort in but I… I didn't know how to or… oh I don't know. I think… it's hard to explain… I just still felt lonely.

From Top

The ensemble 'support' Rob (Tom Marriott) as he recounts his story to Mark.

Section 3 began with a tongue in cheek Quiz Show style presentation, with Mark the Quiz Master (David Thompson). The seated ensemble produced all the SFX of buzzers etc.

Opening movement sequence from *The help – Relief and escape*. Max Petts is lifted to illustrate the 'high' adrenaline rush of initial moment of self-harm.

Director Anna Allen, on Mark's first visit to Solihull, leading the discussion that led to the cast devising the opening physical sequence.

Sonia Oliver Photography

Also from Pping Publishing

The Story Behind Too Much Punch For Judy

The book includes:

- Social and historical background on how and why the play came to be developed including Mark's personal diary entries from that era
- Ideas on how to stage the seemingly impossible accident scene
  Improvisation ideas used to enhance the original performances
- The story of Judy (the person and the play) during, and crucially after, the first production
- Exclusively, the script for the new (2013) prologue framing the original play in a different light, with this question:
  'Can a play change attitudes to drink driving when the subject of the play went on to commit the same offence again?'

"I thoroughly recommend this to other teachers, students, practitioners. It is fantastic to see a resource that will benefit both teacher and student in staging this play. As with 'Drama Schemes,' the book is well laid out, an engaging and insightful read."

Olivia Murphy - Drama and Performing Arts teacher
Bitterne Park School, Hampshire

"This book was enthralling from start to finish. Not only does it give a clear insight into how Too Much Punch for Judy evolved it reminds you of the energy and integrity true drama can bring. Without exaggerating Mark Wheeller's page turner inspired me to give up my leadership duties and get back into the drama studio with my amazing students. Even if you do not discover your Road to Damascus moment you'll be a lot clearer about Too Much Punch for Judy!"

Andy – Drama teacher who reviewed the book on Amazon.co.uk

The Drama Club

by Mark Wheeller and Clive Hulme

This is the record of a project Mark Wheeller never wanted to be involved in - a Junior School Drama Club - but it resulted in a triumph.

Mark takes us through the process of what happened and offers practical advice on running such a project in your own school or club. The book includes a 10 scene, multi-actor script and access to a free online support pack from www.resources4drama.co.uk

It is an ideal source book for those looking for inspiration to run their own extra-curricular Drama activities with children and young people. The innovative guide guarantees parental involvement and appreciation.

"I must admit that when I first opened the package my heart sank, I was hoping for something a little....bigger. Nevertheless, in the old adage of don't judge a book by its cover (or its size), I gave it a read. I have taught drama for over 20 years and although I love my subject, can often get stuck in a rut.
This book gave me a different perspective on how to approach drama with this age range. I was really impressed with some of the new ideas and at their simplicity too. Not only are the ideas there but a 10 scene script. I really am excited about trying out some of the projects in this book and would wholeheartedly recommend it, concluding that size really doesn't matter after all!
Well done Mark Wheeller and Clive Hulme on creating a really different drama book worth every penny".

Coral-Anne Dickinson (from Amazon.co.uk)

Also available from Pping Publishing –
The following Wheellerplays DVDs

I Love You Mum – I Promise I Won't Die

Missing Dan Nolan

Scratching the Surface

Chicken / Chequered Flags to Chequered Futures (double bill)

Too Much Punch for Judy

Bang Out Of Order

Wheellerplays – The Definitive Collection (Double disc)

One Million to STOP THE TRAFFIK

Graham – World's Fastest Blind Runner

***Wheellerplays Exemplified* (Extracts from Wheellerplays)**

Hard to Swallow

If you are interested in purchasing any of these DVDs or books
please contact Mark Wheeller via his web site

www.wheellerplays.com

(note the double L in Wheeller) for further details.